The Minotaur

Libretto

DAVID HARSENT

Boosey & Hawkes Music Publishers Ltd
www.boosey.com

The author, David Harsent, has asserted his moral rights in
accordance with the Designs and Patents Act 1988.

Published by Boosey & Hawkes Music Publishers Ltd
71–91 Aldwych House
Aldwych
London
WC2B 4HN

www.boosey.com

ISBN 978-0-85162-555-3

First impression 2008

Printed in Germany by WEGA Verlag GmbH, Mainz

The Minotaur

an opera

words by

DAVID HARSENT

music by

HARRISON BIRTWISTLE

To Hannah

Acknowledgments

My thanks to John Smith for corrections and suggestions, and –
pre-eminently – to Ruth Padel, who supplied much of the Greek, gave
insightful notes, read the full libretto for faults and flaws, and dealt patiently
with a blizzard of e-mails, all beginning: 'Can I ask you yet again …?'

– *DH*

Characters

Ariadne .. .. Soprano

Theseus .. .. Baritone

Minotaur 1 .. .. Bass

Minotaur 2 (*shadow of Minotaur 1*) .. .. Speaking role

Hiereus .. .. Tenor

Snake Priestess .. .. Countertenor

Ker 1 .. .. Soprano

Keres .. .. Speaking roles

Young Woman .. .. Soprano

Innocents .. .. 2 Sopranos, Mezzo-soprano, 2 Countertenors

Crowd .. .. Chorus

The Minotaur

One : arrival

Crete. A beach. A full moon. Reveal ARIADNE. Downstage is what remains of the wood-and-hide cow Daedalos made for Pasiphae. We see an approaching sail on the horizon: it is black. ARIADNE sees it too. During the course of her aria, two things happen: the ship gets closer until it finally drops anchor a little way offshore; and – slowly – the dawn comes up.

ARIADNE
The moon's an eye that cannot blink or look away ...

I walk this shoreline like a flightless bird.
The sea blots out my footprints, no mark of mine
to show where I came from, no trace of me
except where I stand. How perfect, to live in this moment
with nothing at my back and nothing to face.

The moon's a goddess, though her name's a secret ...

A ship on the horizon, rigged with the black sails of death,
just-visible against the night-sky ...
Each year this ship puts in with its cargo of meat,
the debt that Athens must pay to Crete, the levy of flesh
Aegeus must pay to Minos ...

INNOCENTS
(distant)
Olola ...

ARIADNE
Gull-cry

          their death-song

INNOCENTS
(distant)
Olola ...

ARIADNE
The wind is a tangle of voices, drawn to a whisper ...

The stones on this shore have smooth faces
and tiny, hard hearts. They want to be flawless, they want
to feel the beat of the sea, they want to be washed
clean, scoured by salt. I know what they want.

The wind carries rumours ... I've heard those stories before.

This ship set course for Crete with its burden of souls,
my father's year-in, year-out revenge,
the innocents counting the hours of their lives
like beads on a thread, the mothers' cries
plucked from the air by seabirds and echoed as each sea-mile
brought their children closer to landfall, closer to death.

INNOCENTS
Io moi moi

ARIADNE
Wave-break

          their death-song

INNOCENTS
Olola ...

The ship is closer; the sky carries the first flush of dawn.

ARIADNE
The sea is locks and chains, a door that slams and slams ...

I have walked here night after night, as if each dawn
could be the start of something, as if first light
could bring me to a place I'd never seen – myself
a stranger there and lost to those who love me.

The sea is a rack of bones, a dead man's cul-de-sac ...

Now they are here and the tale is told again.
Blood calls for blood, a debt that's never paid,
betrayal never forgotten or forgiven,
a lust that still festers ...

Now they are here and the game begins.

INNOCENTS
(closer)
Io moi moi

ARIADNE
Dawn-wind

          their death-song

INNOCENTS
(closer still)
Olola ... Olola ... Olola ...

*The ship has weighed anchor a little way offshore, the black sail in evidence.
THESEUS and the INNOCENTS disembark and wade ashore. They stand in
a group by the shoreline: SIX YOUNG WOMEN and SEVEN YOUNG MEN.
One of the YOUNG MEN is THESEUS.*

*ARIADNE crosses to the INNOCENTS and circles the group: she's inspecting
them. She looks hard at THESEUS. Reaches out and touches his hair, his face.
He pushes her hand away. She turns to one of the INNOCENTS and cups that
person's face in her hand, then leans closely, as if imparting a confidence.*

ARIADNE
Blood calls for blood. Nothing changes that.

INNOCENT 1 turns away.

INNOCENT 1
We're the exchange, the sacrifice; we know that.

ARIADNE goes among the INNOCENTS, touching faces, hair and, in some instances, bodies. She's choosing. She takes the hand of ONE OF THE INNOCENTS, who pulls free and turns away.

INNOCENT 2
Our deaths pay a debt, we're settled on that.

ARIADNE
My brother's playthings. Toys for Asterios.

She continues to go among them. Again she picks THESEUS out for special attention. She's puzzled by him. She moves on to YOUNG WOMAN 3, touching her hair, her face. THESEUS pulls the girl back.

INNOCENT 3
We're quittance, we're the payback; we know that.

ARIADNE
Asterios, who likes not grass, but flesh;
not hay but hide; not cattle-cake, but bone.

She moves among them as before, returning, eventually, to THESEUS. She puts a hand on his shoulder, intending just to touch him, as if leaving a mark, but he places his hand on hers and holds it there. She stares at him, then pulls away.

ARIADNE (cont'd)
Not water from the trough, but blood
from the smooth, stained stones of the labyrinth.

They are spoken-for ... they are marked for death.

She is still looking for a victim. This develops into a sort of pursuit-dance.

ARIADNE (cont'd)
I choose …

ARIADNE scans the INNOCENTS, making her choice. She chooses INNOCENT 1.

ARIADNE (cont'd)
… you!

INNOCENT 1
No!

ARIADNE pursues her/him, but the others move to block her and INNOCENT 1 avoids her by going in among them. In this action, THESEUS becomes more obstructive than the others. This annoys ARIADNE, but intrigues her, too. Despite which – or, perhaps, because of which – she ignores his entreaties.

INNOCENTS
Io moi…

THESEUS
I'll go! I'll go alone!

As INNOCENT 1 avoids her, ARIADNE turns her attention to INNOCENT 2.

ARIADNE
If not her – you!

INNOCENT 2
No!

INNOCENTS
Io moi moi …

THESEUS
I'll take her place!

As INNOCENT 2 avoids her, ARIADNE turns her attention to INNOCENT 3.

ARIADNE
So then, it must be you!

INNOCENT 3
No!

INNOCENTS
Io moi moi

THESEUS
I'll go in! Let me go in alone!

Finally, ARIADNE manages to catch INNOCENT 1.

ARIADNE
Yes – you! You will go in first!

INNOCENT 1 turns to THESEUS, uttering his name, pleadingly.

INNOCENT 1
Theseus!

Hearing his name, ARIADNE stops and stares at him. After a pause:

ARIADNE
Theseus …

A moment of confrontation between them, then ARIADNE turns, leading INNOCENT 1 away. The others hesitate, then follow.

THESEUS
Down into darkness …

Now they'll go down into darkness,
into the labyrinth, a place
of one-way streets, wrong turns, blind corners …

These deaths are a debt
that can only be cancelled with a death.

My death, or the Minotaur's, or both ...

The bare bones of the Innocents
litter the black alleys of the maze,
their life-blood cakes the stone,
their cries hang in the air.
Every night, I hear them in my sleep.

My death, or the Minotaur's, or both ...

Only the shedding of blood
can stop this bloodshed ... my death
or the Minotaur's or both,
his bare bones or mine
littering the black alleys of the maze,
his life-blood or mine
caking the stone, his death-cry or mine
hanging in the air.
Every night I hear it in my sleep.

– TOCCATA 1 –

Two : **the choice**

ARIADNE approaches INNOCENT 1 (a YOUNG WOMAN) and puts a hand to her cheek. It would be a fond gesture were it not for the hint of some dark appetite.

ARIADNE
My brother, Asterios: you must go in to him.
Asterios …

INNOCENT 1
… who likes not grass, but flesh …

INNOCENTS
Olola … Io moi moi

THESEUS takes a step or two towards ARIADNE and the INNOCENTS as if he might intervene. She looks at him. Their eyes lock for a moment. Then ARIADNE breaks the look, approaches INNOCENT 2 (a YOUNG MAN) and touches his cheek.

ARIADNE
My brother, Asterios …

INNOCENT 2
… who likes not hay, but hide …

INNOCENTS
Olola … Io moi moi

Again ARIADNE looks towards THESEUS, who has moved closer still. After a moment, she breaks the look between them, as before, and moves towards INNOCENT 3, touching the young woman's face: almost a caress.

ARIADNE
… you must go in to him: Asterios …

INNOCENT 3
… who likes not cattle-cake, but bone …

INNOCENTS
Olola … Io moi moi

ARIADNE looks up. THESEUS has moved closer.

ARIADNE
(to THESEUS)
They are spoken-for … they are marked for death.
(pause)
You are –

THESEUS
Who are –

ARIADNE
– Theseus …

THESEUS
(overlapping hard)
– you?

ARIADNE
You are –

THESEUS
Who are –

ARIADNE
– Theseus!

THESEUS
(overlapping hard: insistent)
– you? Who are you?

ARIADNE
Ariadne. Daughter of Minos and Pasiphae.

THESEUS
Ariadne. Half-sister to the half-and-half.
(*pause*) .
I'll go in to him.

INNOCENTS
(*shared*)
A chance: our deliverance!

ARIADNE
It's not your place.

THESEUS
It's why I'm here.

INNOCENTS
(*shared*)
A trade: a gift!

ARIADNE
You were not one of the chosen.

THESEUS
I choose. I choose myself.
(*beats*)
I came with them from Athens under a black sail.
At the quayside, mothers howled
and beat their own backs and cut their breasts with stones
as the ship made ready, as their children went aboard.

ARIADNE
You cannot choose …

THESEUS
Imagine that. Can you imagine that? – The last embrace,
the last kiss, the last sight of your child
sailing away to die. You stand on the quay and watch the ship
dwindle as it sails towards the sun …

ARIADNE
It's not your choice –

THESEUS
The women leaned together like trees hit by a gale.
Their cries were like the wind in broken branches.
They called on their king but got no answer.
They called on the gods but got no answer
except from Thanatos: 'Your child must die.'
(beat)
I came to take their place. I came to –

ARIADNE
(overlapping)
It's not your choice to make.

THESEUS
Nor is it yours.
(beat)
My father left me a sign – sandals and sword placed beneath a rock
no other man could lift. I wore the sandals, I carried the sword,
I walked from Troezen to Athens. At Epidauros
I killed Corynetes with his own club. Sciron was next:
he fell into his own trap. Sinis was torn
by his own cunning. Procrustes I broke on his own rack.
I came to Athens, then. I stood before my father,
a man I had never seen. I told him I would go to Crete
under the black sail of death. Nothing he said
could turn me from my purpose.
I am here to free them – here to kill or be killed.

ARIADNE pulls a bead from her dress.

ARIADNE
Let this bead decide.
Left hand, right hand – choose.
Let it be chance.

The INNOCENTS are suddenly very interested; if THESEUS chooses correctly, they will be spared. ARIADNE puts both hands behind her back and switches the bead from hand to hand. Then she traps it behind her belt and holds out both hands for THESEUS to make a choice.

INNOCENTS
(shared: in opposition to one another)
Choose the left hand.
Choose the right ...

THESEUS dithers. As he is about to choose, ARIADNE puts her hands behind her back again and pretends to switch the bead from hand to hand. Then she extends her hands once more, inviting him to choose.

ARIADNE
This one or that ...

INNOCENTS
(shared: in opposition to one another)
Choose the right hand.
Choose the left ...

Again, THESEUS is uncertain. Again, ARIADNE hides her hands, pretending to switch the bead, then extends her hands. THESEUS chooses the left. ARIADNE opens her hand. It is empty.

INNOCENTS
(shared)
Wrong hand ... dead hand ...

The INNOCENTS begin to ritually cleanse themselves – something they must do before entering the labyrinth.

THESEUS is angry. He turns on his heel to leave. As he does so, ARIADNE retrieves the bead. THESEUS pauses as if a thought had struck him. He crosses swiftly to ARIADNE and grabs her right hand, intending to prise the fingers open.

THESEUS
Why should I trust you?

ARIADNE opens her hand, revealing the bead.

ARIADNE
This isn't sleight of hand: it's luck, pure luck –
or else the gods decide.

THESEUS holds her look for a moment then moves a little way off to watch events. Although it is now evening and the moon has risen, the sun is still visible in the sky.

ARIADNE
Both sun and moon in the sky, as if time stood waiting …

THESEUS
The gods decide …

The INNOCENTS are staring at the sun and moon.

INNOCENTS (ALL)
An omen …

INNOCENTS (YOUNG WOMAN 1)
Selene will save us!

INNOCENTS (YOUNG WOMAN 2)
We'll keep the moon in sight.

INNOCENTS (ALL)
An omen …

The INNOCENTS begin to move off towards the labyrinth.

INNOCENTS (YOUNG MAN 1)
Helios will be our guide.

INNOCENTS (YOUNG MAN 2)
We'll keep the sun in sight:

INNOCENTS (2 YOUNG WOMEN)
Go with the setting moon.

INNOCENTS (2 YOUNG MEN)
Go with the rising sun.

ARIADNE
Nothing will bring them back.

INNOCENTS (YOUNG WOMEN)
Selene will bring us back.

INNOCENTS (YOUNG MEN)
Helios will bring us back.

The INNOCENTS go into the labyrinth.

ARIADNE
I dreamt myself into the labyrinth –

THESEUS
I dreamt myself into the labyrinth –

ARIADNE
– its smooth white streets –

THESEUS
– its foetid alleyways –

ARIADNE
– its marble walls and sunlit courtyards.

THESEUS
– its dark dead-ends and cross-cuts.

ARIADNE
There were fountains –

THESEUS
There were bones –

ARIADNE
– caged birds –

THESEUS
– and hanks of hair –

ARIADNE
– stone quoits
planted with hyacinth and black hellebore.

THESEUS
– the walls graffitied with blood.

> ARIADNE
> I was lost, but lost to a purpose,
> as if I came closer
> by always moving away –
>
> THESEUS
> I was lost, but lost to a purpose,
> as if I came closer
> by always moving away –

THESEUS
At times the way was so narrow I'd go
like a man on a ledge,
backed up, hands tracking the stone –

ARIADNE
– until I turned once more
towards the centre and all the streets unlocked –
a vast machine unfolding, a puzzle
solving itself, resolving –
a single road that would take me straight to Greece.

THESEUS
 – until I turned once more towards the centre
and all those blank meanders opened up
to give me my first clear sight of the thing.

ARIADNE
And of him – the monster – nothing …

THESEUS
The monster stared at me –

ARIADNE
 – no sight, no sound –

THESEUS
 – and then beyond me.

ARIADNE
 – no hint of harm –

THESEUS
I was something to fear –

ARIADNE
 – no ghost.

THESEUS
 – but not what he feared most.

Three : **the labyrinth**

The YOUNG MEN *come into view: lost in the labyrinth. We hear the* YOUNG WOMEN, *distant, not visible.*

INNOCENT
(in view)
Olola …

INNOCENT
(from a distance)
Olola …

The INNOCENTS *continue through the labyrinth, calling to one another.*

INNOCENT
Olola …

INNOCENT
(a response)
Olola …

ARIADNE
All roads take you closer to what you fear …

THESEUS
Pointless to think of left or right …

The journey of the INNOCENTS *continues, bringing them ever closer to one another. Finally, they meet and move away, going deeper into the labyrinth.*

THESEUS
Olola …

As the INNOCENTS *continue their journey,* THESEUS *stares after them, clearly moved by their plight, then starts to leave.* ARIADNE *calls after him.*

ARIADNE
Theseus …

THESEUS stops, briefly, and looks back at her.

ARIADNE
Forget them. They're as good as dead.

THESEUS
And you, in my eyes, as good as dead …

He walks away, passing the battered structure of Daedalos's cow and pauses to regard it, then looks back, briefly, at ARIADNE.

THESEUS
 … daughter of Pasiphae – whore to the bull from the sea.

THESEUS exits.

Four : **Ariadne**

ARIADNE stares at the model with a mixture of distaste and fascination.

ARIADNE
Daedalos made this: my mother's shame.
(She walks round the cow.)
She climbed inside ...
(She drapes herself over the cow.)
She spread herself like this ...
(She spreads her legs, a lascivious gesture.)
The white bull ... the white bull from the sea ...
the white bull covered her.
The god Poseidon cursed her with this lust.
Cursed her ... cursed my father ... cursed us all.

She gives a great cry. Her body jerks and she throws her head back, as if she, herself, had been penetrated by the bull.

ARIADNE (cont'd)
Ahhhhhhhhhhh .....

ARIADNE slumps a moment, then slides off the frame her hand cupped between her legs. After a beat or two, she recovers.

ARIADNE (cont'd)
She bore a child. My mother bore a child.
Child of the bull from the sea.
The women who saw that birth
never spoke of it except among themselves.

My mother down and howling ... she spread herself ...
(a faint echo of her earlier cry:)
Ahhhhhhhh ....
(beats)

They gave her birthroot and wormwood;
they gave her peony and yarrow.
Two held her in the birthing chair, one knelt to receive ...
(breaks off)
They gave her raspberry leaf and motherwort,
fenugreek and shepherd's purse,
chamomile, geranium, angelica ...

Two held her, one knelt to receive the child,
child of the bull from the sea ...
(breaks off)
One knelt to receive the child ...
(breaks off)
They never spoke of it:
the black muzzle wet from the caul,
the black pelt, the black and bony brow, the horn-buds, the fat tongue
that slapped out at the birth-blood ...
This creature, this half-and-half, this hair-and-horn
humpback, hideous, this child of the bull from the sea ...
(breaks off)
My brother. Asterios.

The INNOCENTS come back into view. They have reached the threshold of the centre of the labyrinth.

Five : **the labyrinth**

The INNOCENTS have reached the centre of the labyrinth. Upstage (or stage right and stage left), slightly elevated, sits a CROWD OF ONLOOKERS (CHORUS). As the INNOCENTS arrive, they are confronted by the MINOTAUR, whose roar combines with a shout of anticipation from the CROWD.

CROWD
Ha!

MINOTAUR
Nuuaaaaargh!

The INNOCENTS scatter.

CROWD
Asterios! Speak!

MINOTAUR
(unintelligible)

CROWD
Man-beast! Hunchback! Speak!

MINOTAUR
(unintelligible)

CROWD
Asterios! Man-freak!

MINOTAUR
(unintelligible)

CROWD
Bull-freak! Say it ...

MINOTAUR
(unintelligible)

CROWD
… say your name. Asterios!

MINOTAUR
(unintelligible)

CROWD
Monstrous! Speak …

MINOTAUR
(unintelligible)

CROWD
… speak your name! Hideous!

MINOTAUR
(unintelligible)

The MINOTAUR rushes at the INNOCENTS. YOUNG WOMAN 1 runs away from the rest and is isolated. The CHORUS chants, some appearing to side with the MINOTAUR, some with the INNOCENTS.

CROWD 1	CROWD 2
This is a road with no end	Go back the way you came
This is a lock with no key	Go back or else you die
Turn that way, turn this	Go with the setting moon
No where to go but in	Between the walls of stone
Turn this way, turn that	Turn this way, turn that
No where to go but on	No where to go but on

One of the INNOCENTS manages to throw his/her cape over the MINOTAUR's head, where it snags on his horns. He is temporarily blinded.

He continues to hunt the INNOCENTS in what becomes a sinister game of Blind Man's Buff.

CHORUS 1
Go in! Go in! Go in!

CHORUS 2
Go back! Go back! Go back!

The MINOTAUR throws off the cape and attacks. YOUNG WOMAN 1 is cornered. The other INNOCENTS scatter and run off into the labyrinth. The MINOTAUR lunges at YOUNG WOMAN 1. She tries to escape but he catches her. He throws her down and penetrates her.

MINOTAUR
(unintelligible)

After the rape, the MINOTAUR nudges YOUNG WOMAN 1 with his horns. She rolls sideways and begins to crawl away, but he blocks her. She half gets to her feet and tries to avoid him, but he blocks her again. Finally, the MINOTAUR rushes at YOUNG WOMAN 1 and gores her repeatedly.

YOUNG WOMAN 1
Aiiiiieee! Io … moi … moi … olola …

ARIADNE
Asterios … all roads lead to death.

The YOUNG WOMAN is dead. The MINOTAUR lies down beside her, sated. ARIADNE and the CROWD sing an Epicedium.

ARIADNE
Her eye loses its light
Her mouth closes on silence

CROWD
Hai Keres ammussoun tas sarkas kai ta ostea

ARIADNE
Youth will come to grief
Love will go to ground
Hope will come to nothing

CROWD
O Thanate, katage paida eis tous Haida domous

ARIADNE
Leave nothing behind
Take nothing with you
To the land of the dead.

The MINOTAUR sleeps.

ARIADNE
After the heat of lust, the heat of anger –
The beast must sleep …

*We hear an unearthly, high pitched shriek. One of the KERES – a winged
female creature with fierce talons – descends and starts to feed on the body of
YOUNG WOMAN 1. After a moment, the creature lifts her head and emits a
raucous cry.*

KER 1
Ruuuaaaaak!

Her soul is mine … her blood is mine …
Death by violence fetches me.
The plague pit, the battlefield,
the murder in the bedroom,
the murder in the nursery.

The KER goes back to feeding.

– TOCCATA 2 –

Six : **the Minotaur dreams**

The MINOTAUR is sleeping. In dream, he confronts a mirror-image of himself. The image is MINOTAUR 2.

MINOTAUR
Daedalos made this:
my road without end,
my lock without a key.
I know all of it, except the path
that leads to the world outside.

MINOTAUR 2
(speech)
The world outside is lost to you –

MINOTAUR
In dreams I seem to remember
sunlight glossing the sea, the sea
breaking on rock, the rock
falling seawards, the scent
of pines and cypresses, a cypress
tipped by the moon, the moon
fading in the rose-pearl light of dawn.

MINOTAUR 2
No. When you dream you dream
only of the labyrinth.

ARIADNE
(off – distant)
Asterios ...

MINOTAUR
In dreams I seem to speak like any man.
I say my name. I tell my story.

I howl the words, I weep the words,
I curse. I call a curse
on love, on love's dark ways.

MINOTAUR 2
Love is lost to you …

MINOTAUR
They bring me these gifts, these innocents …

It seems to me they are chosen for their beauty.
When I see them I have to spoil them,
these creatures too beautiful to live,
their perfect bodies, their pale, soft skin,
my image in their eyes, Asterios, hideous,
reflected in their eyes. I pluck
out their eyes, of course; I rip their skin,
of course; I foul their bodies, of course.

They bring me these gifts of blood …

MINOTAUR 2
Blood calls for blood …

*A second image appears beside MINOTAUR 2. The image is dark, its
features unclear, though we might, from its shape and nature, realise that it is
THESEUS.*

MINOTAUR
Who is that, dark in the mirror beside you?

MINOTAUR 2
No one.

MINOTAUR
A shadow …

MINOTAUR 2
No one.

MINOTAUR
A shadow in the mirror beside you.

MINOTAUR 2
No one.

MINOTAUR
Dark in the mirror – myself
or something like myself, or someone
standing apart to watch, or else
some lost creature from a world of light.

ARIADNE
(off – stronger)
Asterios ...

MINOTAUR
(as if in echo:)
Asterios ...
(beats)
Asterios. Nuuaaaaargh!
I am Asterios: man-bull, half-and-half,
heat in my balls, murder in my eye.

ARIADNE
(off, but close)
Asterios ...

MINOTAUR
(overlapping her)
Asterios ...
Conceived in pain, born in fear,
looked-on with loathing, put out of sight ...

ARIADNE
(entering)
Asterios ...

The image fades as ARIADNE appears in the space. Like MINOTAUR 2, she is a dream-image. The MINOTAUR reacts.

MINOTAUR
What do you want with me? What do you want
when you come to me in dreams?

ARIADNE
Asterios … Are you my clue?
Are you my key to the world outside?

MINOTAUR
Who are you?

ARIADNE
Don't you know your own blood? Blood calls …

MINOTAUR
(overlapping)
… blood calls to blood.
(beats)
Tell me again. Tell me the story of myself.

ARIADNE
Minos went to the Oracle. He asked,
'How shall I prove myself? How shall I prove – '

MINOTAUR
(overlapping)
' – how shall I prove the gods love me?'
The Oracle told him to ask for a sign.
Minos prayed; and the sea-god sent –

He breaks off as a second figure appears alongside ARIADNE. As with the image that appeared beside MINOTAUR 2, we guess the figure to be THESEUS. The MINOTAUR is distracted by it.

ARIADNE
– and the sea-god sent –
(*She is waiting for the MINOTAUR to pick up the story*)
– and the sea-god –

MINOTAUR
(*overlapping*)
Who is that beside you?

ARIADNE
No one.

MINOTAUR
A shadow ...

ARIADNE
No one.

MINOTAUR
A shadow standing beside you.

The dream dissolves. Stage slowly to black.

Seven : **the labyrinth**

The MINOTAUR is asleep. Slowly, the lighting changes from black to dawn-light. The INNOCENTS are in the centre of the labyrinth. The CROWD is calling to the MINOTAUR, nudging him awake with their voices.

CROWD
Asterios ... Wake up ... Wake, Asterios

INNOCENTS
Olola ... Io moi moi

MINOTAUR
(waking: unintelligible)

CROWD
You must wake now ... Asterios ...
Asterios ... Man-beast ... Wake now ...

MINOTAUR
(unintelligible)

In the half-light of dawn, the INNOCENTS are dim shapes. As the light grows stronger:

INNOCENTS
Olola ... Io moi moi.

CROWD
Wake now ... Hunchback, man-freak.

MINOTAUR
(unintelligible)

INNOCENTS
No way out unless we had wings to fly.

CROWD
Look, they are here: your gift of blood.

*The YOUNG WOMEN hold back, but the YOUNG MEN advance on the
MINOTAUR. Since death seems inevitable, they are determined to die bravely.*

INNOCENTS
Left hand, right hand, choose.
Each path brings you back …

MINOTAUR
(unintelligible)

CROWD
Here they are, your gift of flesh …

The YOUNG MEN continue to advance.

INNOCENTS
(a war cry:)
Alalai – alalai – alalai

CROWD
Mismade … mis-shapen … misborn …

*The MINOTAUR advances on the INNOCENTS. The YOUNG MEN hold
their ground.*

CROWD (cont'd)
Unnatural … unpitied … unloved …

*The MINOTAUR continues to advance. The YOUNG MEN also advance
slightly.*

CROWD (cont'd)
Defiler … deformed … defective …
Malformed … malevolent … malign …

MINOTAUR
(*unintelligible*)

CROWD
Speak! Speak! Speak! Speak, freak! Come on, freak! Untie your tongue! Come on dumb beast! Tongue-tied fool!

MINOTAUR
Nuuaaaaargh!

The MINOTAUR attacks. A massacre ensues. The yells of the CROWD and the cries of the INNOCENTS are heard throughout.

CROWD
Kill! Asterios! Kill!

YOUNG MEN
Alalai – alalai – alalai

YOUNG WOMEN
Aaaaiiieeeeeeeeeee!

Finally, the MINOTAUR stands bloody and sated amid the dead and near-dead. Those who are not quite dead make little, helpless movements, perhaps half-raising themselves, or crawling a short way before collapsing. An eerie, livid light on the MINOTAUR and the bodies of the INNOCENTS as ARIADNE and the CROWD sing the Epicedium. The INNOCENTS, in their death throes, sing inter alia:

INNOCENTS
Io-moi-moi ...

ARIADNE
No voice should speak of this,
no song tell of it ...

CROWD
Hai Keres ammussoun tas sarkas kai ta ostea
O Thanate, katage paida eis tous Haida domous

ARIADNE
The sun that shines here is dark
The moon is a blind eye

CROWD
Hai Keres ammussoun tas sarkas kai ta ostea
O Thanate, katage paida eis tous Haida domous

ARIADNE
There is no good day to die
There is no good way to die

CROWD
Hai Keres ammussoun tas sarkas kai ta ostea
O Thanate, katage paida eis tous Haida domous

ARIADNE
Forget the voices still in your ears
As you go down to the hall of the dead

CROWD
Hai Keres ammussoun tas sarkas kai ta ostea
O Thanate, katage paida eis tous Haida domous

The MINOTAUR is sleeping among the dead and dying.

ARIADNE
After such slaughter ... sleep;
Sleep ... and dreams of deliverance.

ARIADNE exits. Now we hear the KERES (offstage). Their voices are soft, but chilling.

KERES *(off)*
Bloodshed fetches us ...
Slaughter fetches us ...

In ones and twos, the KERES enter and walk among the bodies of the
INNOCENTS. One of the KERES utters a shriek and drops down to feed on
a body. Others find the near-dead and rip their hearts from their bodies. The
INNOCENTS scream and writhe as they are eviscerated. The KERES hold up
the dripping hearts.

KER 1
We darkened the sky at Thermopolae,
At Marathon, at Ephesus, at Syracuse ...
We fell like black rain.

We claw the souls from the dead,
we tear the souls from the dying ...

KERES
Starved for blood ...
Ravenous for blood ...

An INNOCENT screams as he/she is eviscerated. A KER holds up the
dripping heart, then proceeds to feed on it.

KER 1
Our talons fast on their flesh
our mouths deep in their wounds
our teeth breaking their bones ...

An INNOCENT screams as he/she is eviscerated. A KER holds up the
dripping heart, then proceeds to feed on it.

KERES
Where hatred brings on murder –

KER 1
(an echo)
Hatred ...

KERES
– where fear brings on murder

KER 1
(an echo)
Fear ...

KERES
– where lust brings on murder

KER 1
(an echo)
Lust ...

KERES
– where rage brings on murder

KER 1
(an echo)
Rage ...

KERES
– where jealousy brings on murder

KER 1
(an echo)
Jealousy ...

KERES
– where greed brings on murder

KER 1 *(an echo)*
Greed ...

KERES
– where madness brings on murder

KER 1
(an echo)
Madness ...

KERES
– where love –

KER 1
– where love brings on murder
our cries are heard, our shadow is cast

An INNOCENT screams as he/she is eviscerated. A KER holds up the heart and proceeds to feed on it; then another does the same; then a third.

KER 1
Their hearts, blood-rich,
their tripes, their lights,
gorge your craw,
feed now, feast now ...

KER 1 descends on an INNOCENT who screams as he/she is eviscerated. KER 1 holds up the dripping heart, then proceeds to feed on it.

KER 1
Ruuuaaaaak!

Another falls on a dead body and tears at it. Another does the same, then two more, then four, then all – their shrieks growing louder, until they fall into a feeding frenzy.

KERES
Ruuuuaaaak! – Ruuuuaaark! – Ruuuuaaark!

– INTERVAL –

Eight : **a proposition**

ARIADNE alone. She turns swiftly, sensing someone's presence. A figure is standing just out of the light but visible. It is THESEUS. He steps into the light.

THESEUS
I will go in to him. I made a promise.

ARIADNE
Then break it: forget you are Theseus, son of Aegeus.

THESEUS
Son of Aegeus …or else son of Poseidon.

ARIADNE
(startled)
Of Poseidon …?

THESEUS
Aegeus was childless. He went to the Oracle
and asked for help. On his way back to Athens,
he stopped for food and rest at the house of Pittheus.
Pittheus had a daughter – Aethra, my mother.

Aegeus spent one night with her; one night only.
That same night, Poseidon lay with her.
She never knew which was my father.
There are those who say I am the son of the sea-god.

ARIADNE reacts, detecting a terrible irony.

ARIADNE
(aside)
And there are those who say
the white bull that coupled with Pasiphae
was really the sea-god in another guise …

If this is true, the monster is son to Poseidon.
(pause: she laughs bitterly)
The gods look down and laugh;
we are their toys, their playthings ...

THESEUS
Aegeus came with me to the ship,
hoping he might turn me from my purpose.
There was fear and loss in his look
but all he said was this:
'If you live, if you return, strike the black sail of death;
make the journey home to Athens
under a white sail. I'll be watching for your return.
Watching for the white sail of deliverance.'

ARIADNE
A sight he'd never see. Even if you killed the creature,
you'd be lost to him for ever in the pathways of the maze.
(beats)
Hoist a white sail. Set a course for Athens. I'll come with you.

This last remark takes THESEUS aback.

THESEUS
Come with me? Why?

ARIADNE
I'm daughter to the man whose arrogance brought shame.
I'm daughter to the woman who sinned against nature.
I'm sister to the half-and-half.
Free me of this. Take me back to Athens as your wife.

He stares at her a moment, then gives a shout of laughter.

THESEUS
My wife! – what do I know of her? Nothing, except
she doesn't look like you, she doesn't speak like you,
she's not a Cretan, and her name's not Ariadne.

THESEUS is standing close to the remains of Daedalos's cow. ARIADNE moves to him. She puts out a hand to stroke his cheek; he turns from the gesture. She moves to Daedalos's model, drapes herself over it and spreads her legs lasciviously.

ARIADNE
Daedalos made this ... Pasiphae climbed inside,
she spread herself, like this ...
(sensually)
Idoo, phlegoh, phlegoh ...

It is a clear invitation to THESEUS. He is aroused and starts towards her, then stops and turns away. ARIADNE has noted his vacillation. She goes to him, taking his arm.

ARIADNE (cont'd)
Take me to Athens with you. Make me your wife –

THESEUS turns to leave.

ARIADNE (cont'd)
– and I'll find a way for you to go in to him –

Hearing this, THESEUS stops and turns to her.

ARIADNE (cont'd)
– and kill him ... and then come back to me.

THESEUS looks at her. She approaches to stand just a short distance from him.

ARIADNE (cont'd)
(intensely)
Kill him ... and come back to me.

THESEUS
You heard what I said!

They confront one another, then ARIADNE kisses him fiercely. He pushes her away, stares at her a moment, then leaves. ARIADNE is distraught.

ARIADNE
The Cretan sky is black, the sun burns black,
a black sea breaks ... O gods, give me Theseus:
give me Theseus and Athens, give me Theseus
and a life beyond this darkness. The labyrinth
is prison to Asterios, Crete is my cage.

If malice will free me, let my mother weep.
If betrayal will free me, let my father curse.
If a death will free me, let the monster die.

A black wind
strikes sorrow off the stones.

Io ... moi moi ...

– TOCCATA 3 –

Nine : **the Minotaur dreams**

The MINOTAUR is sleeping. MINOTAUR 2 enters.

MINOTAUR 2
(speech)
Asterios!
Come up out of sleep in sleep ...

As before, the MINOTAUR confronts what seems a mirror-image of himself.

MINOTAUR
Between man and beast, next to nothing ...

When I sleep, does the man sleep first?
When I wake, does the beast wake first?

MINOTAUR 2
Sleeping or waking, you are yourself alone.

MINOTAUR
The beast's hide and horn,
the man's flesh and bone,
no telling one from the other ...

Except for this lust: all too human
this rage: all too human
this hard heart: all too human
this life in darkness: all too human
this deal with death: all too human
this inescapable sorrow: all too human

MINOTAUR 2
Human, not human ... Asterios, the half-and-half.

MINOTAUR
In this place of despair, this place of silent weeping,
this place of sorrow, of fear, of cries and whispers,
this place of hellish visions, of no way out,
of walls backed up to walls, of black blockades,
I am mobbed by shadows, I'm lost inside myself.

I look through the eyes of the beast to find the man.

MINOTAUR 2
Asterios ... Blood brother to yourself.

A second image displaces that of MINOTAUR 2 – the image of ARIADNE.

MINOTAUR
(to ARIADNE)
Why do you come to me in dreams?

ARIADNE
Why do I dream of you, Asterios?

MINOTAUR
Are you my keeper?

ARIADNE
Are you my deliverance?

MINOTAUR
I am myself alone,
locked in this body, this pelt, this neither/nor,
locked in with my rage ...

ARIADNE
Are you my clue?

MINOTAUR
... despised ... despised ... man-bull, monster, freak.
(beat)
She bore a child. My mother bore a child.

When they cut the cord and put me to her breast
her cry startled the gods.

ARIADNE
Are you my key to the world outside?

MINOTAUR
Minos went to the Oracle.
He asked a question and he got his answer:
'Let Daedalos build a cage without a key,
a place with more dead ends,
more flaws and fault-lines than the human heart.
Let the creature live. Let it live there.'

ARIADNE
(A sudden thought. Aside.)
The Oracle ...

MINOTAUR
Why not smother me? Why not
leave me out to the weather, why not cut
my throat and feed me to the dogs?
Why let me live, except
to remind all Crete of my mother's sin and shame?

Daedalos made this – my cage; my killing-ground.

ARIADNE
(aside)
The Oracle ... Minos went to the Oracle ...

*Now another image appears alongside ARIADNE's – that of THESEUS. It
remains for a brief moment, then fades.*

MINOTAUR
Who is the other one who stands
in the shadow of himself, dark in the mirror?

ARIADNE
No one.

MINOTAUR
In the mirror beside you.

ARIADNE
No one.

The image of ARIADNE dissolves and a second image forms: that of THESEUS, stronger than before.

MINOTAUR
Who is it stands in the shadow of himself?

The image of THESEUS grows still clearer.

MINOTAUR (cont'd)
Who is it with this stony stare, this whiff of death?
(roars)
Nuuaaaaargh!

The MINOTAUR advances on the image, which dissolves. The MINOTAUR seems to step through into darkness. In the same moment, ARIADNE steps out of the dark.

Ten : **the Oracle at Psychro**

A pit opens up centre stage. This is the Omphalos: the centre of the world.
Wisps of gas issue from it. The SNAKE PRIESTESS appears: the voice of
the Oracle. She is bare-breasted and holds a snake in either hand. She is in
a trance. Next to her stands the HIEREUS: his purpose is to translate the
otherwise incomprehensible utterances of the SNAKE PRIESTESS. ARIADNE
enters, carrying a white dove and a knife.

The SNAKE PRIESTESS is uttering a seamless, repetitive, unintelligible,
sotto voce *line. This line is a continuum, uttered by the SNAKE PRIESTESS*
whenever she is not making some other utterance. She breaks off only to warn
or to respond to a question.

SNAKE PRIESTESS
(unintelligible)

HIEREUS
(to ARIADNE)
You have come to the omphalos, the dint of the world.
You have brought your token of blood to the oracle of Zeus.

After the kill the bird must be broken open,
its entrails plucked and spread;
then I'll read the signs and, if they're good,
you'll be granted a single question.

The god speaks through his priestess,
the priestess speaks only through me.

SNAKE PRIESTESS
(unintelligible)

HIEREUS
Now make your sacrifice.

ARIADNE holds the dove aloft, its wings flapping, then cuts its throat. Blood runs down her arms. The HIEREUS takes the bird from her, tears it open, removes the intestines and examines them.

HIEREUS
The liver, blood rich.
The gall, bitter spillage.
The heart's last pulse.

SNAKE PRIESTESS
(unintelligible)

HIEREUS
These omens work in your favour. Ask your question.
The answer comes through me and me alone.

SNAKE PRIESTESS
(unintelligible)

HIEREUS
One question only. Remember that.

ARIADNE
A man enters the labyrinth to face the Minotaur.
He kills the creature … but how does he find his way back?

SNAKE PRIESTESS
(unintelligible)

HIEREUS
Before you get your answer
a question must be asked of you.
Be sure to speak the truth.

SNAKE PRIESTESS
(unintelligible)

HIEREUS
The question is this: why do you ask this question?

ARIADNE
Pity is my reason.

SNAKE PRIESTESS
(unintelligible)

HIEREUS
You have lied. Your question will not be answered.

ARIADNE
Ask me again!

HIEREUS
The moment has passed.

ARIADNE
Remember my father's sin …

SNAKE PRIESTESS
(unintelligible)

ARIADNE
… remember my life-in-shadow.

A pause: as if the SNAKE PRIESTESS were considering this plea.

SNAKE PRIESTESS
(unintelligible)

HIEREUS
Ask, then. But first you must tell the truth.

ARIADNE
Fear is my reason. Fear and anger.

HIEREUS
You have told the truth. Ask again.

ARIADNE
A man enters the labyrinth – once in,
how will he ever return?

SNAKE PRIESTESS
(unintelligible)

HIEREUS
This clew is your clue.

SNAKE PRIESTESS
(unintelligible)

(The HIEREUS hands ARIADNE a ball of twine.)

HIEREUS
This ball of twine.

SNAKE PRIESTESS
(unintelligible)

HIEREUS
Let him go hand over hand –

SNAKE PRIESTESS
(unintelligible)

HIEREUS
– to the centre and back again.
This is all you need to know.

ARIADNE
Will I go with Theseus to Athens?

HIEREUS
One question only.

ARIADNE
(insistent)
Will he take me with him?

HIEREUS
One question only.

SNAKE PRIESTESS
(unintelligible)

HIEREUS
Theseus and Ariadne will set sail for Athens.

ARIADNE
(exultant)
This is all I need to know.

Slowly, the ORACLE descends. She and the HIEREUS are lost in shadow.

ARIADNE
Asterios ... you are the clue ...

An exultant cry. Then, as THESEUS enters:

Eleven : **a blind bargain**

ARIADNE
Theseus and Ariadne will set sail for Athens ...

THESEUS
(wearily)
Why do you flog me with this?

ARIADNE
(crossing to him: eager ...)
I know a way
to send you in and bring you back and leave him dead.
I know a way
to give you what you want ... if you give me –

THESEUS
What?

ARIADNE
A kiss to seal a promise.

THESEUS is uncertain and suspicious.

THESEUS
A promise I haven't made.

ARIADNE
Then go into the labyrinth, go in alone,
go in without help or hope.

THESEUS
What is it, this secret you keep?

ARIADNE
The one sure way ...

THESEUS
The way that brings me back ...

ARIADNE
... yes, back to me.

THESEUS
If I refuse?

ARIADNE
Next year, another ship, another cargo
under the black sails of death:
boys with their wispy beards,
girls with their little breasts as hard as apples,
women at the quayside
tearing at their hair, raking their skin with their nails,
throwing dust in their eyes
rather than watch their children go aboard and –

THESEUS
(overlapping)
Enough! Say what you have to say.

ARIADNE
(reminding him)
A kiss. A promise.

THESEUS kisses her as if wanting to leave a bruise. His next line is an affirmation, but uttered in anger.

THESEUS
Theseus and Ariadne will set sail for Athens!

ARIADNE turns from him in distress, putting a hand to her mouth. Then she recovers and crosses to where the ball of twine lies alongside a short sword. THESEUS hesitates, then follows. ARIADNE hands him the twine.

ARIADNE
Take this and pay it out as you track him: that way

you'll have a line back to the world … back to me.

She takes the sword from the table and hands it to THESEUS.

ARIADNE (cont'd)
No one ever went in to him with a weapon: he doesn't know
what a weapon is, he's never once felt pain.

She puts a hand to THESEUS's cheek: a tender gesture.

ARIADNE (cont'd)
Theseus –

THESEUS anticipates her next remark, though wrongly.

THESEUS
Yes! Theseus and Ariadne will set sail for Athens!
I have said so.

ARIADNE
 – go in to him and kill him.
Kill him and come back … my life depends on this.

THESEUS walks away from her in the direction of the labyrinth.

THESEUS
My purpose here is this: to finish things.
There will be a death, that much is certain.
If the man-bull dies, the debt is written off.
If I die, Minos has a trade: son for son.

*ARIADNE joins him. She holds out her hand. For a moment, THESEUS does
not react to this; then he hands her one end of the twine. As he leaves, the
twine pays out between them. When he is out of sight:*

ARIADNE
Kill him and come back.
Idou, O Zeu.

THESEUS
(off)
Poseidon, I dedicate this death to you.
(beat)
Io dike phaneitai.

Twelve : **the labyrinth**

THESEUS
Io dike phaneitai.

ARIADNE
(off)
Alalai … Idou, O Zeu.

These cries – call and answer – continue as we follow THESEUS's progress through the labyrinth until he comes to the centre. Out of the (relative) darkness, we hear the MINOTAUR. The CROWD is present, as before.

MINOTAUR
Nuuaaaaargh!

CROWD
There comes a day in each man's life
Which is the day of that man's death

THESEUS and MINOTAUR confront one another.

THESEUS
Blood calls for blood.

The MINOTAUR charges. A fight ensues in which they are both wounded. As the fight continues, the CROWD responds to the action:

CROWD
Blood calls for blood
Theseus … Asterios …

The MINOTAUR roars as he fights:

MINOTAUR
Nuaaaaaaargh!

THESEUS
Aéra!

The MINOTAUR staggers back, badly wounded. THESEUS advances, ready to deliver the death-blow. As the MINOTAUR utters his next line, THESEUS hesitates.

MINOTAUR
Ah ....

The MINOTAUR breaks off. He is struggling to become coherent.

MINOTAUR
Whass ...

Yah ...

Pause. The MINOTAUR moves closer to THESEUS. Tries again to achieve comprehensibility.

MINOTAUR
Ehtt ... wauusss ... yah ...

He moves closer still. THESEUS raises the sword as if to strike.

THESEUS
Blood calls for blood.

MINOTAUR
Eht-t-t-t ... wa-a-a-hhs ... yo-o-o-u ...
(breaks through into coherence)
It was you ...
(pause)
You in my dream; you, dark in the mirror –
A man standing in his own shadow ... Who are you?

THESEUS
Theseus, son of Aegeus ... or else
son of the sea-god, Poseidon.

MINOTAUR
The gods look down and laugh ...

THESEUS
Asterios ... Your death-cry or mine:
every night I heard it in my sleep.

MINOTAUR
Now I can speak ... now I am almost human;
now is the right time to die.

*As the MINOTAUR lowers his head for a last, despairing, charge, THESEUS
steps in and drives the sword into the killing-spot between the MINOTAUR's
shoulder blades, leaving the handle protruding.*

CROWD
Aéra!

*The MINOTAUR gives a great roar of agony and staggers forward, clutching
at THESEUS. For a moment, they are in an embrace. Then the MINOTAUR
slips to the ground and slumps back, clearly dying.*

THESEUS
His death lightens my life.
The debt is paid, the bargain broken.

THESEUS turns and starts back, following the twine hand over hand.

Thirteen : **death of the Minotaur**

---

*The MINOTAUR is mortally wounded. He makes a few attempts to reach
behind his back and withdraw the sword, but he's too weak.*

CROWD
Asterios ... Asterios ...

MINOTAUR
(weakly)
Asterios ... I am Asterios ... son of –

*Breaks off as he makes another effort to reach the sword, twisting, groping, but
it causes him too much pain. He falls sideways, roaring.*

CROWD
Son of the sea-god ...

*One of the KERES arrives, though we should not see her come on: just be
aware, at some point, of her presence. Each of the KERES should appear in this
way – a sinister series of arrivals: we should only register the fact that suddenly
there is one, then two, then more, standing a little way off as if biding their time.*

MINOTAUR
Man-beast, the half-and-half, the neither/nor,
here in my cage with no key ... Asterios ... son of –

Breaks off; makes another unsuccessful grab at the sword.

CROWD
Asterios ... Asterios ...

MINOTAUR
Two women at the birthing-chair ... Black pelt, black blood,
black slime from the womb. They never spoke of it.
(Pause. He is weakening.)

One knelt to receive the child of the bull from the sea ...

Breaks off in pain; roars. He is determined to pull out the sword. Makes a mighty effort, withdrawing it, inch by inch. At the same time, the CROWD is leaving, sure of his death.

CROWD
Son of the sea-god ...

MINOTAUR
Asterios ... Son of the sea-god –

He staggers, recovers, then holds the sword aloft. It is running with blood.

MINOTAUR (cont'd)
Son of the sea-god, Poseidon!

The Minotaur sinks to his knees as the CROWD exits.

CROWD
(as they leave)
Between day and dark
                              – next to nothing

Between love and lust
                              – next to nothing

Between heart and hand
                              – next to nothing

Between hand and hurt
                              – next to nothing

MINOTAUR
Born in secret, looked-on with loathing, put out of mind,
gifted with nothing but fury, nothing but lust,
nothing but hatred, nothing but pain.

My world these walls ... no thought of deliverance,

no hope of forgiveness, my dreams always of loss,
(breaks off with – for the first time – a very human cry)
Io moi …

The beast is vile, so the man must go unloved
The beast can't weep, so the man must go dry-eyed
The beast is wounded, so the man must die

Death is the sound of wingbeats and a voice chanting in darkness

He is close to death.

Between womb and tomb
between help and harm
between most and least
between man and beast

Next – to – nothing

The MINOTAUR dies.

In the background, we see the ship, its black sails hoisted, sailing away. The KERES surround the body of the MINOTAUR. Some fall on him and begin to feed; the others move slowly downstage in a ragged group, KER 1 slightly in advance.

When KER 1 is as far downstage as possible, she stops and looks out at the auditorium. She raises her arm and points, her finger travelling in a slow arc to take in the entire audience. Then she gives an exultant, rage-filled, bloodthirsty shriek.

KER 1
Ruuuuuuaaaaaaaaaak!

Stage to black.

– THE END –

Notes

I have moved the omphalos from Delphi to Crete.

I have co-opted the Cretan Snake Priestess as the Oracle of Zeus.

While I have allowed that Theseus might have been fathered either by Aegeus or by Poseidon, I have insisted that the white bull that emerged from the sea and coupled with Pasiphae was the shape-shifted god. In tending to the opinion that Poseidon did, in fact, father Theseus, and definitely fathered the Minotaur, I have made Theseus and Asterios likely half-brothers, thereby completing a tragic familial triangle: Ariadne – Asterios – Theseus.

– DH